Francis

By Griselda Gifford

illustrated by Angela Thompson and Ian Bosworth

Contents

1	The Accident	3
2	The Gypsy's Curse	9
3	In the Lion's Den	19
4	In Trouble Again	31
5	Alice's Sacrifice	41
6	Earning Money	47
7	Meeting Nina	54
8	Threats and Illness	61
9	A Theft at the Hall	69
10	Fire!	78
11	Francis the Hero	84
12	Black Beauty	89

PEARSON
Longman

Text © Griselda Gifford 2004
Series editors: Martin Coles and Christine Hall

PEARSON EDUCATION LIMITED
Edinburgh Gate
Harlow
Essex CM20 2JE
England

www.longman.co.uk

The right of Griselda Gifford to be identified as the author of this work has been asserted by her in accordance with the Copyright, Designs and Patents Act, 1988.

All rights reserved. No part of this publication may be reproduced, stored in a retrieval system, or transmitted in any form or by any means, electronic, mechanical, photocopying, recording, or otherwise without either the prior written permission of the Publishers or a licence permitting restricted copying in the United Kingdom issued by the Copyright Licensing Agency Ltd, 90 Tottenham Court Road, London W1P 9HE.

First published 2004
ISBN 0582 79635 0

Illustrated by Angela Thompson (Advocate) and Ian Bosworth (Advocate)

Printed in Great Britain by Scotprint, Haddington

In memory of my grandfather, David Denton, a blind organist, and of the real "Tommy".

The publishers' policy is to use paper manufactured from sustainable forests.

1 The Accident

One minute there was only the sound of our pony, Tommy, clopping slowly along the road, pulling the cart, and then I heard a loud engine noise. I looked round. One of the new motor cars was coming towards us at a reckless speed!

Tommy, unused to motor cars, trotted faster and laid back his ears in alarm. There was a sound like a gunshot. I caught a glimpse of a man and woman sitting in the front in a cloud of blue smoke, then the driver sounded the horn loudly and Tommy charged sideways into the ditch, tipping the cart over. There was a terrible crack as the shaft and wheel broke and the old pony was on his side, struggling in his harness. My parents and I slid down the side of the cart, Mother still holding the reins.

I yelled at the motor car as it went past, but the driver, his face half-hidden by goggles and a thick cap, did not stop. The car churned up stones and dust as it went. I just had time to see the driver's thick black beard. His passenger, a woman dressed in black, turned and looked at us through her veil. The car left a trail of blue smoke and a horrible smell of oil.

"Help me get your father out, Francis," Mother gasped.

"Poor Tommy!" Father said, as we helped him down. "Is he hurt?"

"I'm afraid he is," Mother said. She looked white and shaken.

When Father was safely out of the cart, I ran to

help Tommy. The old pony reared his head, his mouth foaming, panic in his eyes. Had he broken his leg? It was hard to undo the harness as he was writhing in pain and fear.

I couldn't help crying. I loved Tommy. I had grown up with him and he took us everywhere – for Father's recitals and lessons, for shopping and for picnics on fine days. As I wrestled with the buckles and tried to calm the pony, I thought Father would never get to Ouseford to give his organ recital today. We badly needed the money he was paid. I gulped hard as I saw blood pouring down Tommy's leg where the broken shaft had hit him. I wanted to hit out at those cruel people in the car who hadn't even bothered to stop.

"I can hear hooves," Father said. He can hear better than sighted people can. "Run and see who it is, Francis. They may be able to help."

Coming round the corner was the first of a small procession of brightly painted gypsy vans. The gypsies, who called themselves Romanies, were coming to camp on the common near our village as they did every summer. I stood and waved my arms. Would they stop?

"Please help us!" I called, and the black-haired man driving the first van pulled his horse up. He leaped down when he saw our cart and Tommy on the ground.

"Our pony's hurt," I said, and the gypsy went to Tommy at once, ignoring my parents. He knelt, held the pony's head and breathed into his nostrils. Straight away, Tommy was calmer. Between us, we undid the harness and Tommy struggled to his feet. He stood, shaking, his head down. Sweat covered his body.

Blood was pouring from the cut on his leg. The gypsy took off his bright kerchief and made a pad to press on the wound. He called out in the Romany language and an old woman wearing a many-coloured shawl got out of the van and gave him a flowered cloth, which he tore up and bound tightly round Tommy's leg. My parents thanked him.

The gypsy stroked the pony's head thoughtfully. "Was he frightened by that horseless carriage? It passed us at a great rate, giving our horses a fright."

Father nodded. "It sounded as if it was going much too fast! I heard a rumour that the new owner of the Hall has bought a motor car. But I am sure Lord Bosville would never allow it to be driven so recklessly."

The gypsy muttered something and spat on the road. "A curse on these new machines. Surely they are the work of the Evil One! Now I need to see if the pony's leg bone is cracked." He felt Tommy's bandaged leg, slowly.

I knew horses with broken legs had to be shot; there is no way of saving them. Tommy and the cart is the only transport Father has to his music pupils in nearby villages or to his organ recitals. The only other transport that comes to our small village is a horse-drawn cart, which comes twice a week for those who need to go to Ouseford on market days. Father needs the money he earns from lessons because the vicar, Parson Thornton, pays him so little to play the church organ.

But somehow this didn't seem important.

Tommy's life was all that mattered. Was there anything I could do to help save him? Or to get my revenge on those reckless people in the motor car?

2 The Gypsy's Curse

"I don't think the leg's broken," the gypsy man said at last. "But it's hurt bad. Best he doesn't walk home." By now, all the brightly coloured vans and horses had stopped. Another man came forward and said, "Abe – the pony can go on my wooding wagon. 'Tis empty enough." He touched his cap at Mother. "I'm cousin to Abe Smith. You came to see my baby, Ma'am, last year. Saved her life when the doctor wouldn't come. Look at the baby now." A gypsy woman came forward, holding a child who was smiling and laughing at us.

Mother's white face relaxed and she smiled. "You must be Reuben Smith and baby Rose."

I remembered now, the night she went to the common to see the sick baby. Somehow Parson Thornton had heard of it and in his next sermon he attacked "those folk who encouraged the idle

9

thieving tinkers by giving them medicines and help." I don't like Parson Thornton, who is always frowning and shouting from the pulpit and hates anyone who doesn't come to church.

Father and Mother had been furious about the Parson's sermon. "They're called Romanies, not tinkers," Father said.

Reuben brought his wagon alongside the pony and let the tail flap down. Then Abe tore a strip of cloth and bound it lightly round Tommy's eyes. He stroked the pony's ears and spoke soft words in a strange language. Tommy quietened. Abe put his face to the pony's whiskery nose and blew into his nostrils again.

Tommy stood still, ears back, relaxed, as if sleeping on his feet, as he sometimes did.

The two men led him to the wagon, Abe jumping up first, and two more men came forward to help the pony up the tailboard. Tommy went up quite calmly, as if the gypsy had put a spell on him.

"I'll go with Tommy," I said, jumping up after him.

"Talk to him all the while," Abe said, wedging the pony either side with nets of hay.

"I'll take your folk home in my caravan and we'll be back for the broken cart," Abe said.

Reuben led the big piebald horse pulling the wagon. Tommy shifted nervously, but I stroked his sweat-streaked neck and spoke to him and he quietened as we bumped slowly back to our village.

As we came into Underhill, faces peered through cottage windows. Dr Cutlack drove past in his smart trap looking at us with disapproval.

Parson Thornton was coming out of St Stephen's church as we went past, and he looked grim when he saw us. There would be trouble for Father later for having anything to do with the gypsies.

As we reached our cottage, my brother and sisters ran out and followed as the piebald horse pulled the wagon right up the side track to our little field. Reuben led Tommy slowly through the gate and into his stable. Then he went back to fetch our broken cart on his wagon.

"We can't thank you enough," Father said.

Mother went indoors to fetch the hot water and strips of linen Abe asked for. She took Alice with her because my little sister burst into tears when she saw Tommy's leg.

"What's happened?" my elder brother Albert asked.

I told him the whole story. "Father thinks that Lord Bosville is the only person with a motor car round here."

"I'll kill that driver!" Albert said. "Lord Bosville should know better. I wish I'd seen it, though. I've only seen two petrol motor cars before."

"You mustn't speak like that about Lord Bosville, Albert," Father said. "The car might belong to someone else from further afield."

He used his stick to guide himself up the path to

the house. He didn't hear the old gypsy lady raising her fist and muttering words in the Romany tongue.

"What are you saying?" Aggie, my nosy sister, asked.

"I be putting a grudge on that driver," the old lady said. "And my name's Betsy Smith, young lady."

I felt a shiver going down my back.

"She means she's putting a curse on him," Abe said, his dark face serious.

"He'll suffer, by and by," Betsy said.

Mother came back with the water and linen and I held Tommy's head as Abe bathed his leg. Betsy Smith fetched a pot of herb ointment, which Abe put on the wound. All the time Tommy stood still, as if charmed.

"Don't you fret, young Master," Betsy said to me. A shaft of sunlight through the stable door lit her wrinkled face momentarily, and I stared into her dark eyes. They seemed foreign, mysterious, as if they could see right into my soul. "The pony will mend, but he'll not work again," she said. "Give me your hand."

I did, reluctantly. I didn't really believe all the stories about the gypsies and their powers and yet …

She turned my hand palm up and peered at it.

"I've no silver," I said.

"You'll not need any with Betsy Smith."

I found it hard to understand her accent and sometimes she used Romany words.

"You'll have a long life, not as long as our Queen but you'll live to be as old as me and I'm sixty this year! I see all sorts of creatures and you healing them. You get fearful of things, but before the summer you will risk your life for another. Flames, I see flames ..." And she suddenly stopped speaking. Then she felt in the pockets of her full skirts and put something in my hand. "Keep it to ward off the Evil One."

The object felt hard and furry. I thrust it in my pocket so Aggie didn't see it. Betsy Smith said I would risk my life for someone! Perhaps I would be a hero at last! But I didn't like the sound of the flames. I hoped she was wrong there. I've always imagined myself rescuing someone from drowning ...

My mother interrupted my dreams, returning

with a fruit cake and a basket of apples for our rescuers. "You are Good Samaritans indeed," she said.

"You came out to help Reuben," Abe reminded her. "I'll be back in a few days to look at Tommy."

In the meantime, we had to put fresh ointment on the wound and new bandages each day, and keep him in the stable. The wagon came back with our broken cart and then they were all gone.

"So what was this motor car like?" Albert asked, typically. He's always interested in machines and new inventions. I'd rather have a horse any day.

"Noisy and smelly," I answered. "And you don't notice the details if you're heading for a ditch, stupid! But it had four wheels – and made a tremendous noise. To say nothing of that horn honking at us!"

"I read that the latest motor cars go up to fourteen miles an hour!" Albert was excited.

"I don't care if it can fly! I hate that machine and what it did to Tommy," I snapped.

Aggie and Albert were sent to post a letter written by Mother, explaining why Father had been unable to play the organ that day. I could feel Father's disappointment. He had to learn all his music by heart, with Mother reading it out to him. Now all his hard work had been wasted.

Father felt the broken cart all over with his sensitive fingers. He shook his head. "Too difficult for me to mend."

Alice looked at her worn-out button boots. "I suppose we won't get any more boots now," she whispered to me. "I mean, if Father can't get to his pupils."

"Mine are all right," I said, although it wasn't true. They had been Albert's and now I was growing out of them.

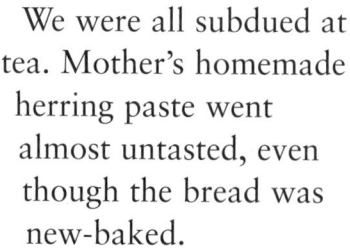

We were all subdued at tea. Mother's homemade herring paste went almost untasted, even though the bread was new-baked.

It was Aggie who said what we were all thinking. "How will Father get to his music lessons and recitals without Tommy? Even if Tommy does get better, it won't be for a while. And what about the cart?"

"Can't we buy a new pony and cart, Father?" Alice asked.

Father told her not to ask so many questions. Then he said grace. My parents did not like to discuss money problems in front of us. I thought that was silly, as we all knew we were poor, although there were some children at school worse off than us, who had no shoes and only a lump of bread for their dinner.

The girls took the dishes to the scullery to wash; Albert said he had school work to do. I was last to leave the room. As I left, I overheard Father talking to Mother: "I don't know what to do. A new pony and cart will cost a great deal of money. It will take months to save enough out of my organist's wages. I won't be able to visit any pupils out of the village either. And we have to feed Tommy in the meantime. We have to buy oats and hay now he can't graze in the field."

I ran back into the room. "Father! Don't have Tommy shot!"

"Please don't interrupt like that, Francis," he said.

"But Father!" I was clutching at his arm, despairing. "He'll get better!"

He patted my shoulder, his square, bearded face very grim. "He may not. But unless he remains in pain, he will not be shot. Now, tomorrow is Sunday and you have the shoes to clean, don't you? And if you want to help Tommy, give him a warm bran mash and fresh straw for his stable."

I went to the boot shelf, sadly thinking about those words, "If he remains in pain …" Then I remembered Betsy Smith's talisman against the Evil One and felt in my pocket.

I held a rabbit's foot in my hand, tied round with a string of dry herbs.

3 In the Lion's Den

I thought about Tommy all the time I cleaned the boots. Usually I grumbled to myself how unfair it was that Albert got out of such a boring job because he had extra school work to do. He's three years older than me and much more clever. He hopes to get into the grammar school; Alice says it isn't fair because she is just as clever but she has to leave school at thirteen.

By the time I had cleaned the button boots Mother and the girls wear on Sundays and the shoes Father wears to play the organ, I was thoroughly miserable.

Cyclops, my cat, watched me through his one yellow eye. He'd lost the other in a fight. He sat beside me in the kitchen as I mixed the mash for Tommy. Mother was busy ironing. She took a flat iron from the top of the range and held it near her cheek, to test its heat. "You did well today,

Francis," she said, smiling at me. "Don't worry too much. Tommy may get better, and if not, Father still has two pupils in the village. He can walk there. And the big cart goes to Ouseford twice a week for people going to the market. Remember the Bible tells us not to worry about the future and to count our blessings."

I could tell she was pretending to be cheerful, so I smiled too and went outside with the bran mash. Cyclops followed me.

Distantly, across the graveyard that separated our cottage from the church, I heard Father practising the organ for tomorrow's service.

"Wait for us!" called Alice and Aggie.

We found Albert looking over the wrecked cart, which was lying beside the stable. "I thought I might be able to mend it with Father's help. But the side's broken as well as one shaft and the axle," he said gloomily.

Tommy's ears pricked when he saw me, and he hobbled very slowly to the stable door.

I held a squashy bit of mash in my hand, under his nose. After a moment, he nibbled at it and I stroked his neck, but he just stared when I put the bucket in front of him. Tears came into little Alice's eyes. "He won't eat and he'll die," she wailed.

"Don't be so silly," Aggie said, briskly raking out the dirty straw and pulling down fresh bedding from the loft. "I'm calling a meeting."

"What about, bossy sister?" Albert asked. There is less than a year between them. They are both quick-tempered and often fight.

"About getting a new pony and cart, of course."

For once Albert didn't argue with her. "That's what I was going to say. We've got to help Father or we'll get poorer and eat nothing but bread and soup." He was stick-thin and always hungry.

"And you'll have to give up going to the grammar school," Aggie said nastily. "Maybe you should, to save money. Parson Thornton's so mean he makes Father pay to teach you Latin."

"You're just jealous and want to be a boy!" he taunted.

"Girls are just as good. Women go exploring in foreign lands now and even become doctors," Aggie said indignantly.

"Don't quarrel, please," Alice pleaded from inside the stable. "It will upset Tommy."

"Could we sell anything?" I asked.

We all thought hard. None of us owned very much.

A small voice came from the open half-door. "I've got something to sell," said Alice. But when we looked at her she wouldn't say any more.

"I know more than the teachers now," Aggie said. "And I'm sick of helping with the infants at school for just a few pennies. I shall leave and get work as a nursery maid."

We stared at her, impressed. She didn't look very grown-up, though. Her big plait had come undone as usual and her grubby white pinafore had a new tear in it, probably because she'd been climbing trees again.

"Why don't we ask Aunt Agnes for the money? She's rich," Alice said. "I heard Mother saying she's coming to see us this Sunday."

"Her good deed of the week to us poor Dentons," Albert said scornfully. "Probably cast-off clothes from the Three Es."

Our rich and loathsome cousins are called Euphemia, Eglantine and Eustace. We call them Phew, Egg, and Useless, or the Three Es.

Mother comes from a rich family. Father used to give her piano lessons. They fell in love but Mother's parents didn't think Father was good enough for her. So Mother ran away from home to marry Father. Since then, her parents have refused to see any of us. They have never given her any money, although we are so poor.

Mother's sister, Aunt Agnes, is the only one who visits us. But she only comes because she feels it is her Christian duty to give us cast-off clothes.

I suddenly felt angry. "But it's all the fault of Lord Bosville's driver. I'll go and tell him what happened. It must have been his motor car; there's nobody else round here rich enough. He ought to pay."

"Father would never let you," Albert said.

I was getting carried away. "I shan't ask Father. I shall just go." I felt excited. I imagined Lord Bosville saying he was sorry and giving me a purse full of golden sovereigns. I could be a hero!

Before I could lose courage, or anyone could follow me, I ran off up the road, past the church to the Hall. As I came to the huge iron gates leading to the drive, the doctor's horse and trap trotted out. The gates were still open so I hurried through and up the long drive to the Hall.

Old Lord Bosville died a few months ago. Now his nephew has inherited the title and the estates and nobody knows much about him.

I stood at the foot of the stone steps that led to the big front door. My legs felt wobbly as I walked up the steps and pulled at the bell.

"What do you want, lad?" asked the footman, giving me a superior look. "You need to go to the back door."

"I'm Francis Denton, the organist's son," I explained. "I would like to see His Lordship on a matter of urgency." I had rehearsed this on the way.

He peered down at me and I tried to look taller. "His Lordship is away."

He looked as if he might close the door so I gabbled. "His motor car caused our pony to bolt and it wrecked our cart and our pony hurt himself too," I burst out. "We need money to replace them."

At the mention of money he turned me away. "His Lordship would never let the new motor car go out in his absence. You must have been mistaken," he said.

"But I'm sure nobody else round here owns a motor car!" I said.

"Then it was someone from miles away," the footman said impatiently, shutting the big doors with a hollow echo.

Something hit my head and I looked up. The top floor window was open and I caught a glimpse of a girl with bright red hair. Then a hand came behind her and slammed down the window.

I bent to pick up the paper-wrapped lump of coal. I smoothed it out and saw a rough ink drawing of a boy with stick-out ears just like mine.

Whoever it was had been drawing me as I came up the drive!

I hurried round to the stable block before the footman came back and sent me packing.

"Who do you want then, Master Denton?" Mr Rust, the coachman and head groom, was coming through the stable archway. I go to school with his son, Horace.

"I want to speak to the driver of the motor car, please."

"James is polishing that contraption they call a

motor car. And he calls himself a 'chauffeur'," Mr Rust said scornfully. "My horses go faster any day. These new engines are nothing but trouble, if you ask me." He tapped his big red nose. "Mark my words, these motor cars will never catch on permanently with all that smell and noise; leastways, I hope they won't or it'll be the death of the horses." He looked at me. "What do you want with James Jackson?"

I explained again. Mr Rust looked surprised. "You say it was this afternoon? I was out exercising one of the riding horses and his Lordship is in London. But I'm sure Lord Bosville wouldn't let the motor car out in his absence. It's new and he's most particular about it – his Lordship's new toy!" Mr Rust said scornfully. "The previous Lord Bosville would turn in his grave to see it!"

I thought that it would be hard to turn over in a coffin.

"I'm overworked, with the under-groom and stable boy ill with the fever, but I'd not ask that James to help. He's a nasty bit of work, a slippery customer," Mr Rust went on. "You'll find him beyond the stable yard, in the coach house, that way," and he waved his arm. "Just watch what you say to that man."

I felt nervous but I walked into the stable yard, holding onto the rabbit's foot in my pocket. The coach house doors were open. A big bearded man was intent on cleaning the white dust off the new motor car. I looked at man and car carefully. The car was the same as the one that roared past this morning, with two seats at the back, two at the front. The light caught the curled brass of the horn. But I couldn't be absolutely sure he had been the driver. It had all been so quick, but the black beard was unmistakable.

"Are you James Jackson?" I asked, trying not to sound nervous.

He straightened up. "You're trespassing, lad!"

"I am not," I said, trying to sound grown-up. "I have just seen Mr Rust. I am Francis Denton, the church organist's son, and I have come to say that this motor car was going too fast and caused our pony to bolt. Now our cart is ruined and the pony's lame. I intend to speak to Lord Bosville about it."

"Come here." He'd rolled up his sleeves and I could see his powerful muscles as he grabbed my chin, jerking it up so I stared into his small dark eyes. "Did your father send you, little boy?" he said.

"No, but …"

His free hand took mine and jerked it behind my back, painfully. "This vehicle has not been out today. So some other motor car made your pony bolt. If I catch you spreading such tales, I know where you live … you understand?"

Now very scared, I nodded. "Get home, little boy!" he said softly and let go of my arm.

I hate to admit it, but I was so frightened of him I ran off. As I passed the Hall, a woman came out of a side door and hurried towards the stable block. She was thin, with black hair and an unpleasant, sour expression. I was almost sure it was the woman who had been sitting beside the driver.

If the motor car hadn't been out, why was James cleaning the dust off it so carefully?

4 In Trouble Again

It was late by the time I got home. Mother said Father wanted to talk to me.

He was sitting very upright in the small front parlour kept for the piano and visitors. "Is that you, Francis?" he asked.

"Yes, Father."

"Where have you been?"

Father hated even the smallest lie. His blindness seemed to have given him the gift of finding out a lie by the tone of your voice, and he often sensed an unpleasant person by their voice, however sweet their words.

I had to tell the truth. "I went to tell Lord Bosville what his motor vehicle had done to Tommy and our cart," I said in a rush. "He should give us money because it was his driver's fault."

"Well?" Father said in a cold voice.

"He's away and his driver denied being out in the machine."

"Francis." His voice was very stern. "You had no right to interfere. We are not absolutely sure it was his Lordship's motor. And if the driver has denied it, that is an end to the matter. I am sure Lord Bosville would not allow him to take the motor car out without permission – nor to drive so recklessly."

"Couldn't we tell the policeman about our accident?"

"The motor car is probably owned by a rich man and he would be believed, not us," Father said. "I shall not punish you this time because you were very helpful when we had the accident. But you will go to your room and not take tea when your Aunt Agnes comes tomorrow."

He turned his head away for a moment and I was sure I saw his moustache twitch as he suppressed a smile. He knew how much I hated Aunt's visits!

"Was he angry?" Albert asked later.

"Yes." I grinned. "But I like my punishment. I'm not allowed to have tea with the horrible Es!"

Mother filled the tin bath by the range for my weekly bath. There was a fruity smell of a new cake baking in the oven. "I'm not to take tea with

Aunt Agnes," I said, and saw the ghost of a smile on her face. She knew how I felt.

As I sat, scrubbing myself with carbolic soap, I looked at the mark James Jackson had made on my arm, and vowed revenge.

The next morning, Father held Tommy's head while I gently unwound the bandage. There was some swelling but I put on more of the gypsy's garlic-smelling ointment and bandaged his leg again. "It looks as if it's healing," I said. "I've heard the Romanies know all kinds of plants and herbs that can cure you."

"I hope so," he said. "Now get ready, it's time for church."

As I took my place by the organ, ready to pump air into it, I saw heads turn. The thin, cross-looking woman I'd seen at the Hall came into church with a girl of my age. I could just see the red curls under her hat.

Behind them came the nursemaid, old Charity Woods, holding a small child. They all went to sit in the Bosville pew.

The sides of the box pews were high, but from my perch by the organ, I saw the girl trying to shift away a little from the skinny woman, who put out a gloved hand and held her arm tightly.

"Francis!" Father hissed and I pumped for all I was worth as he played. If I stopped pumping, the music would stop too.

Albert, who was in the choir, sang a solo. His voice was so angelic you would never imagine him in one of his tempers.

I guided Father back to our pew at the side of the church to listen to the vicar's sermon. Alice was nervously biting at the ends of her kid gloves. Mother sat very still and upright.

The pews were so high in front that we couldn't easily be seen, so I leaned towards Aggie, who always knew the village gossip. "Who's the red-headed girl and the skinny woman?"

"I think the girl is Lord Bosville's daughter, Nina, and the woman is Miss Crabtree, her governess," Aggie whispered back. "She looks as sour as crab apples, doesn't she?" and she giggled.

I forgot all Father's teaching about forgiving our enemies and stared at Miss Crabtree, hating her. I was sure she had been in the motor car and had seen us in trouble and not stopped the driver.

"Thou shalt not steal," Parson Thornton boomed from the pulpit. "And take care, the thieving gypsies have returned to our village. They have no Christian conscience, taking poultry and killing pheasants with their slings – from His Lordship's estate, no less! And I am warning you, good people of Underhill, that your soul is in peril if you allow a gypsy to tell your fortune …"

I wanted to stand up and shout out that Abe Smith had helped us, like the Good Samaritan Parson Thornton preached about so often. And I didn't feel guilty at having my fortune told.

The owner of the dairy, Mr Clay, came up to Father after church and said he had heard our pony had been injured. He offered to ask his veterinary surgeon to call.

"Please, Sir," I said, despite Mother's warning looks. "One of the gypsies has treated our pony."

"Francis!" Father said, annoyed. "Be quiet! It's very kind of Mr Clay."

As I moved away, I heard Mr Clay say, "Parson's right; you can't trust those gypsies."

I was worried when I heard the veterinary surgeon was coming. Supposing he thought Tommy should be shot?

After lunch, I checked on Tommy. He was standing with his head low, and for the first time I realised that he was old, as well as injured. I talked to him and then sat on a bucket in his stable, looking through the half-door at the wild clouds tearing through the sky.

Aunt Agnes arrived at teatime in her smart carriage, drawn by two shining black horses. They were frothing at the mouth, probably from the tight reins they wore to keep their heads so high and arched. Father said it was a cruel practice.

Our three cousins walked solemnly behind our aunt, who was dressed in the very latest fashion with a big hat smothered in feathers; I almost expected to see it fly away! Egg and Phew, the twins, both paper-pale and fair, walked hand in hand, wearing blue silk dresses and capes trimmed with fur. Fat Useless slouched behind them, carrying a large parcel. I guessed that it held their beastly old clothes for 'the poor Dentons'.

IN TROUBLE AGAIN

"You have a straw in your hair, Cousin Froggy," Useless said, sniffing. He always had a running nose. It was bad enough having to wear his old clothes, which were usually too big for me, but hearing my nickname was worse. Some of the boys at school use it, as well. It's not my fault that my eyes are very big and green. I hate the nickname but Alice says it reminds her of a favourite book, *Froggy's Little Brother*, which always made her cry.

"Eaten any good flies lately, Froggy?" Useless said. I held my tongue, as I wanted his family on our side.

As we came into the cottage I heard Mother telling her sister about the accident.

"How unfortunate," Aunt Agnes said. "But

that pony must be quite old – I remember you getting him before my twins were born. I never keep old horses. They lose their strength and go so slowly – whipping just them makes them fall and break their knees. You will just have to get a new horse and cart." Did she imagine we could use magic?

I went up to her. "Aunt Agnes," I began, and then faltered as she turned to stare at me out of cold blue eyes. "Please listen." I touched her silk-covered arm. "We can't afford a new horse and cart. Would you help us?"

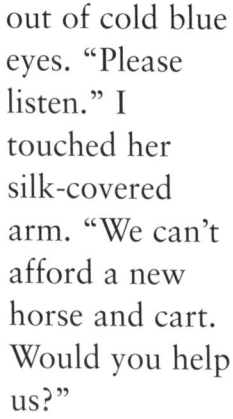

There was a dreadful silence and I could hear my heart thudding.

Then Aunt Agnes gave a gasp and Mother said, "Francis, that is very rude and forward of you," and Father sent me to my room, forgetting I was going there anyway as a punishment.

I sat on my bed, staring out of the window, wanting to knock Aunt Agnes' hat off her smug head. The scudding clouds were grey now and the wind was blowing the petals off our big apple tree.

When Aunt Agnes and the cousins had gone, my brother and sisters came to see me. "She went on and on about your bad manners," Aggie said. "She'll never help us now."

"You shouldn't have asked her for help," Albert said.

"Mother says we must not ever talk about being poor," Alice said. She was clutching her only doll, Evangelina. "Egg and Phew laughed at Evangelina because her nose is chipped and she's lost some hair. They have six china dolls, a rocking horse and a dolls' house with handmade furniture and real pictures. It isn't fair!"

"But just imagine having Aunt Agnes for a mother!" Aggie said.

Alice looked horrified and we all laughed.

Mother came in to say Father wanted to speak to me before evensong. Was I always to be in trouble?

"You must learn to think before you speak, Francis," Father said. "Do you realise that you shamed us in front of your aunt?"

I said sorry but I couldn't help adding, "But I thought she might help."

"We would not ask for charity from anyone. Now, get ready for church. There is to be no more talk about the accident."

In church that evening, my thoughts were like angry bees in my brain, and I was hard put to keep pumping the organ bellow. Like the others, I had an idea for earning money. And I was going to expose James Jackson as a liar.

I remembered his hard hand gripping my arm and his threats, and shivered. It was going to be hard to be a hero.

5 Alice's Sacrifice

When we came down for breakfast a soapy-smelling steam oozed into the kitchen from the bubbling water in the copper. Mother was doing the laundry, pounding at the simmering clothes with a dolly stick.

I bolted down my porridge and went to give Tommy hay and to look at his leg. He'd somehow got the bandage loose and by the time I'd done it up I had to run to school, way behind the others. When I saw Aggie ahead going through the girls' door I wondered if she'd really persuade our parents to let her leave school.

I was worrying about Tommy and my plans, so I didn't hear Mr Thomas when he asked me a question. Then I used my dip pen carelessly and somehow sprinkled ink over Horace Rust's writing as well as mine. Mr Thomas picked up the cane.

"Francis didn't do it on purpose, sir," Horace said. "He wasn't looking."

"Be quiet!" Mr Thomas ordered me out in front of the class. I tried not to flinch as he struck the palm of my hand very hard with his cane, three times. Afterwards, I found it painful to hold the pen.

"He got you to jump, Froggy!" jeered huge Charlie Crowe, after lessons were over. "You're going blind like your father!"

I went for him, headbutting. For a moment I took him by surprise. He reeled back, but recovered and pushed me over so hard I was winded. Albert charged at him like a whirlwind, arms flailing the air, and Charlie ran off.

My friend Horace Rust panted up, coughing. He's been ill a great deal and is always short of breath. "You are brave, going for Charlie like that. You know how many times he's called me names! And I'm sorry you had the cane on account of my book."

I brought out a handful of marbles and we found a quiet corner of the yard to play in.

Horace said, "Father reckons your pony must have been scared by some other motor car, from Ouseford or the like. His Lordship's new motor car hasn't been out of the grounds yet as far as he knows. That's what I want to do when I grow up, drive a motor car for a rich gentleman. Only I daren't tell Father. He thinks horses are best."

I thought of my plan. "Does your father need help now his stable boy is ill? I want to earn money after school and on Saturdays."

"Yes, he's short-handed and mother says I'm too poorly to help out. I'll tell him you want work. But he might have to ask Lord Bosville first."

As we lived so close to the school, we Dentons ran home for our lunch. I hurried along with Albert, who seemed unusually quiet. Aggie came pounding up, red-faced. "Alice didn't come to school," she said breathlessly. "I thought she'd gone ahead of me but she wasn't there when Miss Banks called the register. I said she was ill."

"Maybe she stayed behind to help with the washing," I suggested. Alice loves helping in the house, and I know she hates the rowdy school yard.

But Mother asked as soon as she saw us, "Where's Alice?"

Our lunch forgotten, we searched the house and garden, even Tommy's shed. "Let's see if anyone in the village has seen her," I suggested, and we ran off down the road. Most people were out working in the fields, but we asked two old ladies sitting in their doorways. They shook their heads.

When we came to the village green we saw Betsy Smith carrying a basket, about to knock at a door. I ran up to her. "Our sister Alice – small, dark hair – have you seen her down here?"

Betsy Smith smiled at me. "I seen her, getting on the cart going to Ouseford with a parcel. How's the pony faring?"

"The wound's healing up." I wondered where on earth Alice had been going in Ouseford. She was too young to be travelling on her own.

"Keep on with Betsy's salve." She clutched my arm. "You still got the rabbit's foot? That's St John's wort round it to keep away the Evil One. Watch that little one, Alice. She's so good and kind that the Evil One wants her for himself, for always."

"What does she mean?" Aggie asked as we walked on.

"And why would Alice be going to Ouseford?" Albert asked at once. "And where did she find the money for the fare?"

"Probably she still had that florin Aunt Agnes gave each of us at Christmas. She never buys anything from the pedlar when he calls," Aggie said.

We went back to tell Mother and Father. They both looked upset. "What can she be thinking of?"

Father said, "She's only nine years old."

"I do hope she's all right," Mother said. "I shall meet the carrier's cart when it gets back."

We ran back to school, nibbling hunks of bread and dripping as we went. "She's probably trying to get work or something silly," Aggie said.

I worried all the afternoon. Supposing Alice

got lost? Or met a gang of rowdy lads? Or went off with a stranger? She had only been to the town with us a couple of times.

We were all there, on the green, when the cart packed with people jolted slowly into sight. Alice jumped off and burst into tears when she saw us.

"I did it to help!" she said, and thrust a purse into Mother's hands.

6 Earning Money

"You went to the pawnshop with your books!" Father repeated, as if he could not believe what he heard.

Alice was still crying. "Yes. *The Fairchild Family*, *Black Beauty*, *The Daisy Chain*, *Froggy's Little Brother*, and ..." She gave a gentle moan. "My Sunday School prize, my lovely *Home Words for Heart and Hearth* with those wonderful pictures."

Black Beauty was one of my favourite books too; in fact, I'd given it to Alice.

Father asked Mother to take us on ahead. Then he linked his hand in Alice's. "We shall talk on the way home."

Later on, Alice came running out to join us by Tommy's stable. "He wasn't really angry," she said. "He said he didn't want me to make such a sacrifice and we must pay the shop before the month runs out and the books are sold."

"It was noble of you," Albert said, and Alice looked pleased.

We were all in the stable and I was putting some more ointment on Tommy's leg when I heard Father's stick tapping on the path as he felt his way along.

He held the top of the half-door to the stable. "Are you there, Francis?" he asked.

"Yes, Father," I said.

"We all are," Alice chimed in.

"I thought you'd like to know that the veterinary surgeon came this morning," he said. "Apparently the tendon sheath in Tommy's leg is damaged and he will always be lame. He said if the pony were his, he would shoot it." We all gasped in horror. "But I said we would keep Tommy unless the leg refuses to heal."

I let out my breath in a great sigh.

"Father," Albert said. "I would like to leave school and get work."

"No, Albert," Father said. "You show great promise and will go to the grammar school."

Albert opened his mouth and shut it again. I could tell he wanted to argue, but Father looked so stern and definite, there was no point.

I was filling a bucket of water for Tommy when Horace Rust came to our door. "Father says you can help him with the horses after school if your parents agree," he said.

I took Horace with me. Father was playing the piano but he

stopped, his hands resting on the keys. "Father, it's me," I said. "And Horace Rust. You know I would like to work with animals when I leave school, Father. Well, Horace's father is short of help. Both the under-groom and stable lad have the scarlet fever."

"He would earn sixpence a day, Mr Denton," Horace said. "More on Saturdays."

Father thought for a moment, then he nodded. "Provided you work really hard, Francis and don't neglect your school books."

When we were eating our late tea, Aggie shared some gossip she had heard about the Hall. "It's so sad that those children at the Hall have lost their mother. She died only a few months ago. Charity Woods was engaged as a nurse when they came to the Hall last month, but really she's too old to manage a baby of two and a high-spirited girl of twelve. The governess, Miss Crabtree, has just been taken on, but I hear she is unpopular and also gets very angry with the children."

"We must pray for the family, my dear," Father said.

I wasn't going to pray for the uncaring Bosvilles, but then I imagined a world without Mother, her quick step, smiling face, bright blue eyes and curly black hair that was always escaping from its pins, and I felt sorry for the children.

After tea, I answered a knock on the door. It was Parson Thornton's wife, collecting for our great Queen Victoria's Diamond Jubilee. There were to be all kinds of celebrations because nobody else had ever ruled a country for sixty years.

"For the fireworks?" I asked. I was particularly looking forward to the fireworks and bonfire.

"No. It is to be a present for our dear Queen herself from the people of Underhill."

I saw Mother give money we couldn't afford.

"Why give a rich Queen a present?" I asked my mother afterwards. "Wouldn't it be better to give money to beggars?"

She smiled at me. "In some ways I agree with you. There is a big difference between rich and poor and many suffer. But our Queen's long reign has made Britain great, as you know." It didn't feel that great right now, but I knew better than to argue.

I was helping Father dig up new potatoes when Albert came running, with Aggie behind him. "Father – the doctor's delivery boy has scarlet fever. It's spreading round the village. I've been to see Dr Cutlack and he can give me work to do after school, wrapping up medicines and delivering them. Please say yes."

Father leaned on his spade. "You didn't tell him about our accident?"

"No. But the money will help us."

Father sighed. "You are good children. Tell the doctor you can help for a while, but you still have to do your Latin translations with Parson Thornton."

It was Aggie's turn then and she boldly asked Father if she could leave school. "I know all they can teach me," she said. "And I don't want to be a schoolteacher. For now, I shall look for work with children until I am old enough to be an explorer."

I realised Father was really worried about money when he agreed.

"Guess where I'll look for work?" she said to me later. "At the Hall! I'm sure if Lord Bosville hears of our trouble he might help, even if the car wasn't his. After all, he could probably buy us ten ponies and carts and not even notice it!"

I wondered if I should tell Aggie that I was sure the chauffeur was lying and that I was determined to find out what had really happened. Then I reminded myself that my elder sister was too bossy. She'd take over my idea. I needed to do this myself.

7 Meeting Nina

Aggie came to school next day carrying a letter from Father – written by Mother, of course – to say Aggie would be leaving at once. "Will you come with Horace and me to the Hall after school?" I asked her.

She shook her head. "No. Better that the staff don't see me with you. I shall try to see the housekeeper and tell her that I know the nursemaid, Charity Woods. And I shall bring a letter from the school to say I have been minding the young children for some time. I shall get the position, you'll see!"

She left school for ever at midday and went up to the Hall. When she hadn't returned by teatime, Mother said perhaps she was already working.

Horace Rust came for me and we walked up the road towards the Hall. As we passed the church, Parson Thornton was walking out of the gate. "Ha! Young Denton!" he said, ignoring Horace. "I am about to visit your parents. I heard when you had your unfortunate accident you allowed a gypsy to help you. It is most unwise. They are thieves. Lord Bosville's gamekeeper says the gypsies are stealing pheasants."

I thought the pheasants would be shot in the autumn anyway by Lord Bosville and his friends just for sport. At least the Romanies took them for food.

"We would have been hard put to get home without the Romanies' help, sir," I said.

Horace touched his cap politely. "Maybe old Obediah, the poacher, took them birds, sir. That's what my dad reckons."

Parson Thornton frowned at him. "The gypsy

camp is an eyesore on the common, and I hope you boys keep well away from the ungodly people." He marched off angrily.

The gates to the Hall were shut but we went through a side entrance.

I looked round nervously for James Jackson but the coach house doors were shut. We found Horace's father in the stables. He said he could pay me three shillings and sixpence a week, if I worked all Saturday.

Horace went to the Rusts' cottage to help his mother with his six little brothers and sisters while I was shown the horses. Their coats shone with grooming and their big brown eyes looked at me inquisitively. But they were much larger than Tommy and I felt a little nervous.

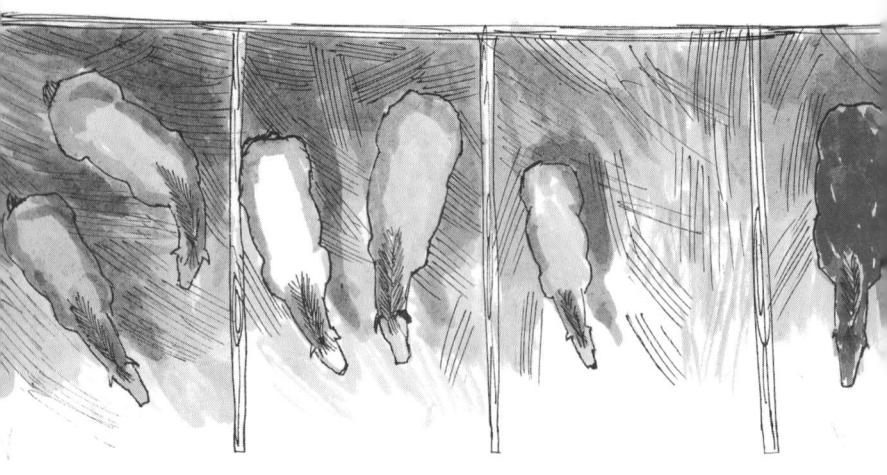

The carriage horses were called Juno and Jupiter. Mr Rust told me they were friendly, so I went into their loose boxes and gave them bits of apple and carrot I had brought from home. Then the two old horses in the next loose boxes, Thornbird and Raven, nuzzled me and I began to feel happier.

"And this is Miss Nina's new pony, Merrylegs," Mr Rust said. "Your first task is to saddle him ready for her ride this evening. Then you will clean his loose box." Merrylegs – that was the name of a pony in *Black Beauty*. Nina must like the book too.

I heard a high, trumpeting whinny from the end of the stable and saw a flash of chestnut through the barred upper door of the last loose box. "What's that horse?" I asked.

"That's Prince, the stallion. When the old Lord Bosville took ill last year, he sold the mares but he couldn't bear to part with Prince. I take him out for exercise, but he's quite a handful! Come and see him."

Prince snorted and trotted round the loose box, his neck arched and his tail high. "Part Arab, he is." The horse came up to the groom and delicately took a piece of apple from his palm. Then a girl's voice called loudly, "Is the pony ready for me?" and Prince's eyes rolled as he shied away. "Miss Nina. Don't call so loudly. He's a nervous horse," Mr Rust said.

Nina was dressed in a dark purple riding habit, which made her red hair look even brighter. I knew she must be the girl who had dropped the drawing on my head. I took my cap off reluctantly.

"Francis Denton is coming to help out," Mr Rust said.

She grinned. "Your sister Agnes is playing with my tiresome baby brother while old Charity sleeps over her tea. No doubt she's put a drop of gin in it." I felt pleased that Aggie had been taken on in the nursery.

"I know I'm early but I had to get away from my horrible new governess. She's always cross; I think she hates children. I really miss my old governess and our home in Germany. I wish Father had never inherited the title. This place is just too big." She sighed.

"You drew a picture of me," I said.

She giggled. "Good, wasn't it?" She saw the ladder leading to the hayloft, tucked up her long riding skirt and climbed up. "I'll look about while you get Merrylegs ready," she called down.

I fumbled with the girths and bridle. I was used to putting Tommy into the shafts but we had only ridden him bareback round the field. Merrylegs puffed and I swear took in air to his fat stomach as I sweated to tighten the girths. There was a giggle and I looked up. Nina was looking down at me. "You're no stable boy, are you?" she taunted.

When Merrylegs was finally ready and Nina was coming down the ladder, covered in hay, an angry voice behind us shouted, "You are a disobedient girl, running off before your work was finished."

Miss Crabtree stood menacingly in the doorway. She looked at me through narrowed eyes. "Have I seen you somewhere before, boy?" This was not the time to talk about the accident, so I kept quiet.

Miss Crabtree tried to grab Nina's arm, but she sprang away shouting, "Leave me alone! I shall tell my father I don't like you when he returns from London."

I had never heard a child speak so rudely to an adult before, but I couldn't help admiring Nina's spirit. Then I had another of my brilliant ideas.

8 Threats and Illness

Mr Rust saddled up the old hunter and took Nina out with Merrylegs on a leading rein before I could speak to her.

It was hard work mucking out the loose box, and it was suddenly very quiet. I wished Horace would come back and see me. After I'd cleared the stone floor I began to spread fresh straw with a fork. A voice made me almost jump out of my skin. "So now I know where to find you!"

I turned round to see James Jackson in the doorway.

"I wonder you dare show your face here!" He stepped forward and with one swift movement pulled the hay fork out of my hands. Then, grinning horribly, he thrust the prongs at me. I forgot all about being brave and backed away. "Remember, if you say one word about the motor car, I'll find you. Boys can easily fall out of hay lofts. Do you understand?"

I nodded dumbly. Then he was gone, striding off. I sat down on an upturned bucket and remembered Betsy Smith's words about being a hero. I just wouldn't let that terrible man frighten me off. I threw straw about fiercely, but I was very glad when the horses clattered back over the cobbles.

"What's wrong? You look as if you've seen a ghost," Nina said.

There was no chance to say anything to her because Miss Crabtree came hurrying into the yard, looking flustered. "You're late, Miss Nina!" she hissed angrily. "Come in at once or you will go to bed without supper." Then she darted a nasty look at me. "You – boy! Your sister is waiting for you on the front steps."

Nina was scowling furiously as Miss Crabtree dragged her off by the hand, like a tiny child.

"I feel sorry for Miss Nina with that woman!" Mr Rust said. He inspected my work, said I'd done well and could go.

Aggie couldn't stop talking as we walked down the long drive together. "The housekeeper used to work for the old Lord and she's really friendly. Charity is far too old to be a nurse to Master Alexander. He's two years old and he cries because she's got him so bundled up in clothes he can hardly breathe, and she won't let him run around. Then she went to sleep in her chair so I took him into the garden. I took his boots off and let him run on the grass."

"Did you see Nina? She came to the stables."

"She had nursery tea with us. She kept making me laugh because she imitated that dreadful Miss Crabtree. Luckily Charity is so deaf she couldn't hear her." Aggie swung from a low branch by the drive. "Oh, and I told her about the accident. She's going to tell her father when he comes back at the end of the week."

"That was my idea!" I shouted. "And I can see your bloomers!"

When we got back, Alice was mending a sheet and Father was playing hymns in the front room, but Mother made cocoa and asked us how we had got on. Albert was very excited. "I'm definitely going to be a doctor," he said. "I'm learning already about mixing medicines. Dr Cutlack let me help. Then I delivered the bottles and pills.
I was allowed to bring the bicycle home. It's not like our old boneshaker with solid tyres. It's got rubber tyres you pump up and it just glides along!"

"You're lucky," I said enviously.

"I wish I had a job with a bicycle," Aggie said wistfully. "But I like the children."

I told them about the stable, but I didn't mention James Jackson because I had been a coward.

"Do you think we'll have saved enough to buy a pony and cart by the time of the Jubilee?" Aggie asked.

Mother smiled a little sadly. "It's very helpful

THREATS AND ILLNESS

to have the extra money – but a pony and cart cost a great deal. Your father has had two more invitations to give recitals for the Jubilee, but I have to write to refuse and to tell Father's more distant pupils he cannot get there."

"Don't!" Aggie said dramatically. "Please wait a few days." And she winked at me.

There was a knock at the door and I went to answer it. It was Abe Smith and his old mother, come to see Tommy.

"Tinkers! Dirty tinkers! Thieving tinkers!" Two boys were shouting from their perch on the wall opposite. By the fading light I saw they were Charlie Crowe's elder brothers. My heart thudded, but I shouted at them to go away.

65

When they saw Albert behind me, they ran off.

Mother gave the Smiths some homemade beer and oatcakes.

"Thank you, Ma'am," Abe said. "You're the only people in this village ready to smile at us. Others are throwing stones at our womenfolk when they sell pegs and baskets. We'll not come this way next year; there's other places that treat us better."

Old Betsy Smith beckoned to Alice and took her hand. "You have a kind heart but a weak body," she muttered. "You have a fever, child."

Mother felt Alice's forehead and told her to go up to bed. "She needs my herbs for her fever," Betsy said. "Send the boy to fetch a potion tomorrow." Mother thanked her, but I wondered if she would use unknown medicine on Alice. I hoped it wasn't the typhoid fever that had blinded Father and killed even the Queen's husband, Prince Albert.

We went outside with Abe, into the dusk. I lit a lantern so he could see Tommy in the dark stable. Abe took off the bandage and felt Tommy's leg, saying it was healing well.

"The veterinary surgeon came and said we should shoot him, but Father refused," Albert said.

"Don't let the vet near him," Abe said. "I'll bring him out and see him walk." He stroked Tommy's head and breathed into his nostrils, muttering something in the Romany language. The pony came out of the shed, obedient as a dog.

It was very sad to see him limping so badly. I heard Father's stick tapping up the path. "Is it you, Abe?" Father asked.

"Yes, Sir. The pony's healing well, but I fear 'tis not likely he'll pull a cart again," Abe said.

We went back to the house silently, feeling very sad.

Later, Mother went up to see Alice and said she was afraid it might be scarlet fever. Alice was the only one of us who hadn't caught it two years ago.

After that, none of us felt like talking. Alice was delicate, always catching colds, wheezing and coughing in the winter. I felt a shiver of fear.

9 A Theft at the Hall

Mother said Aggie would be better sleeping on her own, especially as she was going to look after the baby at the Hall – just in case there was some way of carrying the illness. So Aggie was to sleep in the parlour on an old feather mattress.

I heard footsteps and coughing in the night, and Mother looked very tired in the morning. "I was right about it being scarlet fever. Her poor face is bright red with the rash," she said.

"At least we know it is scarlet fever and not typhoid fever," Father said. "That's even more dangerous, as you know from my experience."

"For Alice, it could be serious," Mother said quietly. "She has so often been ill. Albert, will you run to the doctor's and ask him to call?"

Aggie wanted to stay and help, but Mother said she must be reliable or the Bosvilles would find someone else in her place. Albert caught up with me and we went to school in sad silence.

When we got home at lunch time, Mother was upstairs with Alice. Father said the doctor thought Alice might be getting pneumonia. "He wanted to bleed her!" Father said indignantly. "He was annoyed when we said she was too weak."

Albert and I decided we couldn't face afternoon school. He quietly went off to the doctor's to do extra work, but I guessed he would ask Dr Cutlack about Alice.

Somehow I had more faith in Betsy Smith's potions. I went past the Hall and up the track to the common.

The gypsy camp was at the top, near a dew pond. Shaggy horses and ponies looked up as I came near, a couple of goats grazed on long tethers and lurcher dogs looked at me suspiciously, one growling. I have never been scared of dogs, so I stood still and put out my hand. The fiercest dog came up to me and let me pat his shaggy head.

Barefoot children stared at me and a woman was stirring something in an iron pot suspended over a fire. "Betsy Smith?" I asked, waving at the brightly-painted vans. She pointed, smiling and showing a mouth empty of teeth.

Betsy Smith was sitting in the doorway of her

van. She smiled when she saw me. "You want my cure for the little one's fever?"

She went inside the van and came out with two small stone jars. She pointed at one marked with a cross. "Ointment for the rash. A spoonful every three hours from the other jar for the fever." Then she took my hand in hers. "Take care. Danger – from the dark man." She added words in the Romany language. "Go back quickly."

Father looked worried. "She's worse," he said. I hurried upstairs. Mother was sponging Alice's face. I showed her the pots and explained the doses. "Well, we can try. She can't keep the doctor's medicine down." Alice opened her eyes but didn't seem to see me.

Mother managed to get Alice to swallow a spoonful of the potion and she put the cream on the bright red rash. "We have to pray for her now," she said. "See to Tommy and then you must go to the Hall. I hear Mr Rust's baby son is ill too."

When I got to the stables, I asked after the baby. Mr Rust looked worried. "I'll be going back to the cottage to see how he's faring," he said. "In the meantime, you can clean the coach harness and the saddles. His Lordship comes back soon. It's to be hoped he'll want to travel in the coach, not that motor contraption." He hurried off.

I tried not to think of illness and death as I sat in the open doorway, cleaning the harness. So many people lost their babies to illness. And supposing delicate Horace caught the fever?

A dark shadow loomed over me. I looked up and saw James Jackson scowling down at me. I froze. "Remember, boy!" he growled as he walked away.

A moment later, I saw Miss Crabtree, walking

swiftly past. Her head was partly covered with a shawl but I would know that bony figure anywhere.

When Aggie met me to go home, she asked how Alice was.

"No better," I said gloomily.

Neither of us talked as we went home.

When Mother came downstairs she said Alice seemed to cough less. "But she is still very sick."

None of us felt like eating a lot at tea – not even Albert.

I tossed and turned that night, running in my dreams from the huge dark figure of James Jackson, who caught me and covered me with a black cloak. I fought for breath and I must have yelled because Albert gave me a shove to wake me up.

I was tired then and slept late. I splashed water on my face from the jug, dressed and ran downstairs. Aggie had already gone to the Hall.

Mother sat at the table, looking white and tired. She tried to smile at me. "Alice is sleeping now. I hope ..." and she tailed off.

"I think we should have the doctor again," Albert said. "Who knows what the gypsies put in those potions of theirs."

"You're as bad as Parson Thornton!" I shouted at him. "Look how they helped Tommy."

Father told us to be quiet and get to school. We took bread and cheese, as Mother would be too busy with Alice to get lunch.

It was a long day and I could not concentrate. Mr Thomas made me stand in a corner with a dunce's hat on my head, but I was too worried about Alice to care.

We ran home full of dread. Betsy Smith was coming out of our gate. "How is Alice?" I asked, fearing the answer.

"Turning the corner," she said, smiling.

After this good news we had a good appetite for our tea. But as we were eating, Aggie charged in, still wearing her apron.

"They won't believe me! Charity Woods has sent me packing because I argued about it. They're after the gypsies ... Alexander ..." She collapsed in a chair, red-faced, her hair coming down.

Mother gave her a drink of water and Father told her to explain what she meant.

"There's been a theft at the Hall and they're blaming it on the gypsies! And Master Alexander went missing and was found by Betsy Smith, and now the nurse and Miss Crabtree say Betsy was taking him away, not bringing him back."

It took a while to sort out what had actually happened because Aggie was so upset. Charity, the nurse, had gone out in the garden with Alexander, leaving Aggie to wash the children's clothes and tidy the nursery. As Miss Crabtree had a headache and was resting, Nina insisted on showing Aggie some of her mother's jewellery, taken from a chest in her father's study.

"She put a diamond and emerald tiara on her head and a necklace to match," Aggie said.

"Nasty old Miss Crabtree came in, very angry, and snatched the jewellery from her to put it back. Then I went to find the nurse and Alexander for their lunch. I found her at last, asleep on a bench by the lodge gates and the baby carriage was empty! Alexander had obviously climbed out – he was too old for it, anyway. When I woke her, Charity said she'd only dropped off for a minute." Aggie looked scornful. "A minute! More like an hour, I'm sure. We called after Alexander and then I saw the door at the side of the big gates was open. His wooden horse was lying on the road." She paused for breath.

"Go on – what happened?" I asked.

"I saw Betsy Smith walking up the road, with Alexander in her arms."

"So Charity must have been pleased," Mother said.

"No – she claimed Betsy had stolen the baby and was taking him to the gypsy camp. And she told the housekeeper and steward. Then a footman found an open window in the study, the place in a mess and the chest open. The emerald tiara and necklace were missing!"

"So have they called the police?" Father asked.

"Yes, and Miss Crabtree said that while I was looking for Alexander she saw Abe Smith running through the park. They're going to arrest Abe and his mother!"

Before my parents could stop me, I ran outside. I jumped on Albert's bicycle and pedalled up the road. I had to warn the gypsies!

10 Fire!

I passed a group of boys, including the Crowes, walking up the road. They carried sticks. "You tell those gypsies to go or we'll make them!" they shouted.

This made me pedal even faster and I was panting by the time I reached the common. Abe was sitting with a crowd, by the ashes of the fire.

"The police ..." I gasped. "There's been a robbery at the Hall and the governess says she saw you in the grounds."

His black eyes were hard. "And your sister – did she say my mother stole the child?"

"No – no – it was old Charity Woods, the nurse. She'd fallen asleep and Alexander wandered off. She had to blame someone else. And there's a crowd of boys walking up the road, with sticks."

Abe spat contemptuously into the remains of the fire.

"That's what I think of Underhill village. We'll go back to our winter quarters near Ouseford, where folk accept us. We were going to surprise the village with a fair for the Jubilee but not now."

He strode off with the other men, fetching the horses. They would soon be harnessed and the wagons and vans would leave the village, for ever.

Remembering I still had a job to do at the stables, I went back. At the crossroads, I met the Crowes and their gang. "The gypsies have gone," I told them.

Charlie Crowe ran after the bicycle and grabbed at my shirt. "You're lying!" he shouted. I just pedalled on, feeling his weight dragging until the shirt tore. He yelled as he fell on the road.

When I reached home, everyone seemed cross with me until I explained why I'd gone. Albert snatched his bicycle and pedalled off for the doctor's. I changed my torn shirt and went back up the road, this time to the Hall.

When I got to the stables they were deserted. I was wondering what to do when Horace Rust came panting along. "My father's sick too now, and the baby's no better. I've got to get back to help Mother. Father says will you get the hay down and give the horses their oats. Then the carriage horses need mucking out and grooming, ready for His Lordship's return." He looked really upset. "I'm sorry you have so much to do, Francis." Then he walked home, coughing and white-faced.

I had never worked so hard before. I cleaned out Juno and Jupiter's loose boxes, tying them up first by the iron rings. Then I groomed them, spending time on their flowing manes and tails, for the old Lord Bosville would never have horses' tails docked, as so many did.

The wind swirled round the buildings and the grey clouds outside made the dusk seem to fall sooner. I felt very much alone. Supposing James Jackson came along, to polish the motor car? I told myself I had just to be brave and stand up to him, but I was scared. I patted my pocket to be sure the rabbit's foot was still there.

I took the feed buckets round to each horse, then I mounted the ladder to the hayloft and threw down hay into each iron manger. Suddenly I felt very tired and lay back for a rest on the soft hay.

I must have fallen asleep for a moment because I was woken by voices below me. "Don't fear, James, my own darling. That stupid boy has gone home." Miss Crabtree must be talking about me! "The policeman has gone after the gypsies. Wasn't I clever to say I saw one of them running off?"

There was a pause. I moved so that I could see what was happening. Miss Crabtree and Jackson were kissing! "Wonderful clever, you are," Jackson said. "So where are the jewels?"

"Here, in this leather bag.

We just have to hide them. If we disappear today they might be suspicious. Besides, the policeman is coming back to see his Lordship as soon as he comes home tomorrow. Then he may search our quarters when they can't find the jewels at the gypsy camp."

Jackson grunted. "Nobody will think of a stable. Then, when all the fuss is over and the gypsies are arrested, we fetch the jewels and disappear! You've done well, sweetheart." He laughed and opened the door to Prince's box. There was a great clattering and whinnying.

"Take that, you brute!" Jackson shouted. "The beast bit me!" The stable door slammed.

I was so pleased I nearly fell through the trapdoor. Then I heard Miss Crabtree talking from Merrylegs' loose box. "Here – I have the place. There's a loose brick under the hay rack. Hand me the jewels."

If only Mr Rust was here with me! There was nobody to prove what I had heard and I dared not come down and confront the thieving couple.

They kissed and hugged each other, talking in low voices. After a while I smelled smoke and saw Jackson had a cigar. "His Lordship's," he said, laughing.

Then Miss Crabtree said she had to go. "We can't afford to make them suspicious."

"I'll get back to that wreck of a cottage his Lordship so kindly gave me," Jackson said. "But when we've sold the jewels, we'll live like grand folk. I shall buy a new motor car for us to drive."

I waited until their footsteps had died away. Then I smelled burning. Smoke rose from Prince's stall. He whinnied and I heard his hooves clatter.

I saw flames creeping up the top of his stall. Jackson must have thrown his cigar butt into the horse's stall, straight on the fresh, dry straw.

"This is it, Francis," I told myself. "Time to prove you're a hero!"

But I wanted to run away.

11 Francis the Hero

The smoke was making me cough and choke, so I came down the ladder and ran as fast as I could past the flames which were licking up the side of Prince's box. The other horses were getting alarmed now, whinnying and moving about.

I could only fetch one bucket of water at a time. By the time I'd gone for help Prince might be dead and the fire would have spread. I had to get the horses out.

I tore off my shirt, doused it with water from the yard tap and tied the sleeves round my nose and mouth before facing the black smoke. Merrylegs was trotting round the loose box agitatedly. I spoke to her and managed to catch her halter to lead her out to the yard.

Prince stood at the back of his box, his ears laid back, trying to escape the small greedy flames that were eating away at the wooden side of his box. I called to him but his eyes were wild.

I remembered the fire in *Black Beauty* when the groom tied his scarf round the horse's eyes to get them out of the stable. But how could I get near the frightened horse? I had to hide my own fear first so I could calm him. I went along the far side of the box, away from the fire, holding out my hand and talking softly to him but he backed away.

I took the wet shirt from my face and sprang at him, grabbing his halter and throwing the shirt over his head. He reared up, carrying me with him, but I hung on, talking to him and he came down, shaking all over. I tugged frantically at the halter. Prince wouldn't move. Then I remembered what Abe Smith had done. I reached up and breathed into the stallion's nostrils, half expecting to be bitten. But he snuffled back, and when I pulled at the halter he moved at last and I led him to the yard.

When I went back, I realised too late that he'd still got the wet shirt over his head so I was soon choking on the thick smoke. As I plunged on, it seemed as if I could see Betsy Smith's dark, wrinkled face through the swirling smoke and hear her voice. "Creep low, under the smoke," she was saying, so I crawled to the other stables.

Juno and Jupiter were easier to get out, because one followed the other. I had to put my shirt over Thornbird's head and Raven followed him through the choking smoke. Coughing, I fell to my knees on the cobbles.

I heard men shout and then I knew nothing.

When I came to, I was wrapped in a couple of old

sacks and propped on the far side of the yard. The horses had gone. Mr Rust, white and ill-looking, said the servants had taken them out of the stable yard. The fire engine, pulled by two strong horses had already arrived and the fire was dying down to smoke and small flames. I coughed and wheezed beside Mr Rust, who shook with fever. We watched the firemen subdue the fire with water until there was just a hissing from the smouldering wood.

Mr Rust pulled me up. "Come to the Hall, Francis," he said hoarsely. "You've saved the horses, lad."

My brain seemed to be fuddled with shock and smoke and I tried to remember something I had to do.

"Jackson and Miss Crabtree stole the jewels," I gasped. "Hidden in Merrylegs' box."

"Show me." He followed as I staggered on jelly legs to the blackened and waterlogged stable. Nina ran out from a crowd of servants who had come to watch.

"Francis! You saved the horses! You're a hero!" she shouted.

Someone was calling her, but she followed us into the reeking and charred stable, now covered with smouldering planks from the loft floor.

I pointed to the iron rack, filled with blackened and sodden hay. "Below – move the brick." Then my legs gave way and I had to sit on the wet floor.

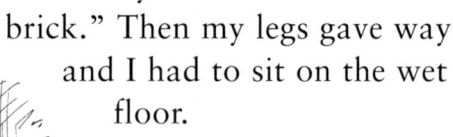

Nina darted forward and I heard her shout, "Mother's jewels!" before I fainted again.

12 Black Beauty

"There's someone to see you, Francis," Mother said.

It was the day after the fire. The doctor had given me medicine that made me sleep so deeply that when I woke I wondered if I had imagined the fire. But my hair smelled of smoke and my arm hurt where I'd hung on to Prince's halter. I sat up. "Did they arrest James Jackson?" I asked.

"They did," said a tall, red-haired man as he walked into the room. He had a friendly face and bright blue eyes. "And Miss Crabtree."

"This is Lord Bosville, Francis," said Mother.

He smiled at me. "You saved my horses. You are a very brave boy. And Nina tells me that the thieving James Jackson drove my new motor car without permission and at a reckless speed, causing you to have an accident. I should never have hired the fellow. It's my fault, entirely. When you are better, perhaps tomorrow, I shall send my carriage to bring you and your parents to the Hall."

Alice smiled weakly. It was the first day she had been allowed to get out of bed. The others crowded round telling me how brave I was. I lay back, remembering how terrified I had been. "I was scared," I admitted to Aggie.

"But if you aren't scared, then it's not being brave, is it?" she said, and I suppose she is right.

The next day I felt better and Lord Bosville sent his carriage to collect Father, Albert and me. It was driven by the groom, who had recovered, as Mr Rust was still ill with scarlet fever. Mother stayed with Alice and of course Aggie was working at the Hall again.

The horses pulled the carriage quickly up the hill. I supposed they had already forgotten the fire. They were lucky; I would always remember it.

"I wonder what he wants us for?" Father asked.

"Do you think he'd show me his motor car?" Albert asked eagerly.

We passed the Rectory. Parson Thornton was just coming out and I saw his head turn and his mouth fall open, when he saw who sat in the open carriage.

The horses trotted up the long drive at a great rate. They stopped before the steps to the front door. All the servants were lined up outside. I saw Charity, the nurse, with Aggie holding Alexander by the hand. Lord Bosville stepped forward and waved his arm. "Three cheers for this brave boy!" he said and they all cheered.

A footman helped Father down and Lord Bosville came over to talk to him.

There was a light clatter of hooves coming from the stables. My heart beat faster as I saw Nina driving a cart, pulled by a black pony. They stopped in front of us and Nina's father held the pony's head.

"This pony and cart are for you, Mr

Denton," Lord Bosville said. "Please accept my apologies for your accident and my thanks to your son for saving my horses."

Father ran his fingers over the front of the cart and then stroked the pony. His eyes filled with tears, then he frowned.

"I cannot ..." he began, but Nina called out, "Please, Mr Denton, please accept the gift, sir. It is not charity. It is what we owe you. And my papa wonders if you would teach me to play the piano?"

Of course she won him over. "I would be very pleased to teach you," Father said. "And I thank you, Lord Bosville, for this generous gift."

"Has the pony a name?" I asked. I would always love Tommy most but I had to admire the pony's shining black coat and alert head. "I believe he's called Blackie," Nina said.

"But he must be Black Beauty!" we said, almost together, laughing.

Then Albert asked if he could see the car, and

Lord Bosville himself drove it from the coach house with Albert beside him, red-faced with excitement. They drove along the drive and back. Albert said afterwards that they had reached twelve miles an hour! And on the return journey Albert and Lord Bosville had changed places and Albert was driving!

This, I thought, is the happiest day of my life.

"They're lighting the bonfire now!" Aggie shouted. It was the evening of Jubilee Day and we were all in the field behind the church. The

Romanies had come back to the common and had brought their friends to run the fair. Lord Bosville had sent word to them at Ouseford that they would be welcome again. He must also have spoken to Parson Thornton, because he no longer ranted against them.

The scarlet fever epidemic was over; Alice was gaining in strength. Horace's baby sister and father had recovered, and the whole Rust family came to the fair on the common.

Father played at three organ recitals in Diamond Jubilee week and we all had new boots. He had gone back to teaching his old pupils, and Nina enjoyed the lessons so much that Father's fame spread, and he was asked to visit two more wealthy homes to teach the piano.

Alice looked so well we had almost forgotten she'd been ill – and Mother drove Black Beauty to Ouseford to redeem her books from the pawnbroker.

When Aunt Agnes and our cousins came to see us, they seemed impressed by the new pony and trap, and by Father's titled pupils. "They're just snobs," Aggie said scornfully.

Useless said to me, "So I suppose you're a hero now, Froggy – who would have thought

it!" Albert gave him
a great push, so
fat Useless
knocked over
Egg and Phew.
We Dentons
laughed so
much we
nearly collapsed too! But Aggie said later,
"Francis was very brave. He really is a hero."
I felt really proud.

Albert continued to work for Dr Cutlack
when he could, but he went on studying for the
grammar school. Aggie went back to school but
she often came to see Alexander, who now had a
capable new nurse.

"Just imagine – every village in England will
be lighting a bonfire!" Aggie said.

"And fireworks. They'll be setting them off
soon," Albert said.

"I shall watch from the window with
Mother," Alice said.

"And I shall imagine them from the time long
ago when I could see," Father said, a little sadly.

I slipped away quietly to the ponies. Tommy
and Black Beauty came up to the gate, Tommy
walking stiffly.

"I've come to keep you company," I said.

I went into the field to give them both apples and sugar lumps. Then I led them into the stable, so they wouldn't be scared by the sounds and sight of the fireworks.

Tommy nuzzled my face, so his whiskers prickled my skin. He was still lame, but he enjoyed bossing young Black Beauty about, getting first to the feed buckets every time.

"I'll always love you best," I said. Tommy whinnied gently, as if he understood.